The 2015 Synod

The Crucial Questions:

Divorce and Homosexuality

Geoffrey James Robinson

By the same author:

Marriage, Divorce and Nullity -
A Guide to the Annulment Process in the Catholic Church (1984)

A Change of Mind and Heart:
the Good News According to Mark (1994)

Travels in Sacred Places (1997)

Confronting Power and Sex in the Catholic Church:
Reclaiming the Spirit of Jesus (2008)

The Gospel of Luke: For Meditation and Homilies (2012)

Love's Urgent Longings: Wrestling with Belief in Today's Church (2010)

For Christ's Sake End Sexual Abuse
in the Catholic Church for Good, (2013)

The 2015 Synod

The Crucial Questions:

Divorce and Homosexuality

Geoffrey James Robinson

ATF Press
Adelaide

Catalyst for
Renewal Inc.

2015

National Library of Australia Cataloguing-in-Publication entry

Creator: Robinson, Geoffrey, 1937- author.

Title: The 2015 Synod : the crucial questions : divorce and

             homosexuality / Geoffrey James Robinson.

ISBN: 9781921511103 (paperback)
             9781921511110 (hardback)

Notes: Includes index.

Subjects: Divorce--Biblical teaching.
            Divorce--Religious aspects--Christianity.
            Homosexuality--Biblical teaching.
            Bible and homosexuality.
            Homosexuality--Religious aspects--Christianity.

Dewey Number: 241.63

All biblical quotations are taken from the NRSV.

Cover design by Astrid Sengkey
Layout - Chris Powell, Lane Print and Post

Text Minion Pro Size 11 & 12

Published by:

An imprint of the ATF Ltd.   Catalyst for Renewal Inc.
PO Box 504   PO Box 265
Hindmarsh, SA 5007   Swansea, NSW 2281
ABN 90 116 359 963   www.catalyst-for-renewal.com.au
www.atfpress.com

To the victims of abuse, the divorced, the homosexuals,
to all women, and to all others
within the Catholic Church who have not been treated
as Jesus would have treated them.

CONTENTS

INTRODUCTION

The recent session of the Synod of Bishops (October 2014) sought to look at the modern family through a pastoral lens, so it had a particular concern for situations where there seemed to be a conflict between Church doctrine and pastoral need. Two subjects rose to prominence.

One concerns the situation of Catholic persons who have grown up to discover that their natural sexual attraction is as lesbian, gay, bisexual or transgender persons. The doctrine is that any sexual act other than one between a man and a woman within marriage and open to procreation is disordered and mortally sinful. The pastoral need is that heterosexual marriage is not an alternative for such people and yet they feel not the slightest call to the life of total celibacy that this teaching would demand of them under pain of eternal punishment.

The other concerns the plight of Catholics whose marriage has failed and who have later remarried. The doctrine is that marriage is indissoluble, so the couple are held to be living in an ongoing and mortally sinful situation. The pastoral need is that such people feel that they are permanently excluded from Communion and the Church.

Many speakers at the Synod tried to find pastoral solutions within the doctrinal teaching, but it must be said that they did not have much success. Some strenuously opposed such attempts, insisting on the full rigour of the teaching.

It seemed to me that the majority were entirely genuine in their concern to meet the pastoral need, but believed that any pastoral solution had to be within the strict bounds of the doctrinal teaching, and did not really know where to go.

I suggest that if the second session of the Synod in October 2015 is to find answers, it must first look seriously at the Church teachings involved to see whether they might allow some 'room to move' in finding pastoral solutions. That is what I shall seek to do here. I am not seeking to impose one understanding, but to show that there is more to these two subjects than can be contained in the current stark teaching of the Church.

Allow me first, in a prologue, to give a brief context.

Prologue

1

A God of Infinite Patience

Science tells me that the world began with a Big Bang;
faith tells me that this Big Bang was an explosion of God's love.

I cannot offer scientific proof of this faith belief,
but it is the most satisfying explanation I can find
of all that I see around me,
both in the material universe and within my own heart and mind.

At first vast amounts of energy swirled in the cosmos,
and then, over immense periods of time,
more solid objects began to form,
as stars, planets and galaxies came into being.
This world had its great beauty and majesty,
but there was no thinking and feeling being there
that could respond to the love that had created it.

More billions of years passed,
until on the planet we inhabit
the first primitive life forms came into being,
then crawled out of the sea and began to colonise the land.

An extraordinary and beautiful variety of plants and
animals developed,
but there was still no being that could consciously respond to
God's love.

At last a few animals began to stand upright on two feet
and develop their conscious lives.
Human beings slowly evolved who could think and feel
and, finally, respond to God's love.

From the explosion of love in the Big Bang
to the first conscious response to God's love
had taken the scarcely imaginable time of 13.8 billion years,
and over all that time God had
waited . . . and waited . . . and waited,
not interfering, but,
with infinite patience,
allowing things to develop at their own pace.

There were many attempts by human beings
to understand the origin and meaning of this world,
though the earliest attempts usually involved nothing more
than stories of warring gods and superhuman heroes.

Then the people of Israel came to believe in one God
and they developed and wrote down a story of their moral and
spiritual journey.
The journey began with ideas of superiority and vengeance
(Gen 4:17–24),
but then gradually rose to ideas of respect for the dignity of others
and the rights that flow from this dignity (Ex 20:1–17),
and from there to ideas of loving one's neighbour as one loves
oneself (Lev 19:18),
and even to loving as God loves (Deut 6:4–9; Jonah 4:9–11).

There were almost as many steps backwards as forwards,
but the story of this moral and spiritual growth mirrored the
growth in nature.

A person named Jesus then came from God,
taking everything that was good from this story,
but also taking the story further
by showing the world a degree of love
that reflected the original explosion of God's love in creation.
The hope was that others would imitate this love
and the process of development might accelerate.

God has waited all this time for the level of growth
we have achieved
and, if necessary, will wait for as long again for the full working out
of the divine plan.

I suggest that the final goal of the divine plan
is that the human race should continue to grow
in moral and spiritual stature
until it in some manner returns the world to the love
from which it came.
I have no idea what form this will take,
but I believe it is the final goal of the human race.
If it takes another fourteen billion years or more,
then so be it, for God can wait.

Jesus Christ lived a mere two thousand years ago,
an instant in time compared to the billions of years of creation.
And God can wait as long as is needed
for the followers of Jesus to develop and apply his ideas
in such a way that the whole world
may develop more securely towards its final goal.

All the evidence would indicate
that we are still in the very earliest days of the Christian story,
as it becomes part of the story of the whole human race
in its quest to return the world to the love from which it came.

2

The Teacher

He never taught a lesson in a classroom.
He had no books to work with,
no blackboards, maps or charts.
He used no subject outlines, kept no records, gave no grades.

He spoke of planting crops, catching fish,
baking bread, or cleaning the house,
drawing his lessons from the familiar.
He told simple stories that could be endlessly applied.

His students were the poor, the lame, the deaf, the blind, the
outcast,
and his method was the same for all who came to hear and learn:
he opened eyes with faith,
he opened ears with simple truth,
he opened hearts with a love born of forgiveness.

He delighted in seeing his students gradually grow
towards all they were capable of being.

His first teaching was always that of personal example,
as he lived the lessons he taught to others.

A gentle man, a humble man,
he asked and won no honours,
no gold awards of tribute to his expertise or wisdom.

And yet, this quiet teacher from the hills of Galilee
has fed the needs,
fulfilled the hopes
and changed the lives of millions.
For what he taught brought heaven to earth
and God's heart to all.

3

The Song

In everything he did and in everything he said,
Jesus Christ sang a song.

Sometimes, when he cured a sick person, he sang softly and gently,
a song full of love.
Sometimes, when he told one of his beautiful stories,
he sang a haunting melody,
the kind of melody that, once heard, is never forgotten,
the sort of melody you hum throughout the day
without even knowing that you are doing it.

Sometimes, when he defended the rights of the poor,
his voice grew strong and powerful,
until finally, from the cross,
he sang so powerfully that his voice filled the universe.

The disciples who heard him thought
that this was the most beautiful song they had ever heard,
and, after he had returned to his Father,
they began to sing it to others.

They didn't sing as well as Jesus had
–they forgot some of the words, their voices lacked force
and went flat–
but they sang to the best of their ability,
and, despite their weaknesses,
the people who heard them thought in their turn
that this was the most beautiful song they had ever heard.

The song gradually spread out from Jerusalem to other lands.
Parents sang it to their children
and it began to be passed down
through the generations and through the centuries.

Sometimes, in the lives of the great saints,
the song was sung with exquisite beauty.
But at other times and by other people it was sung badly,
for the song was so beautiful
that there was power in possessing it,
and people used the power of the song
to march to war
and to oppress and dominate others.

So the song was argued about, fought over,
treated as a possession, distorted,
and covered by many layers of human additions.
And yet, despite everything human beings did to it,
it was still capable of captivating people
whenever its sheer simplicity and aching beauty
were allowed to pierce through.

One of the last places the song reached
was a land that would later be called Australia.
At first the song was sung there very badly indeed,
for the beauty of the song was drowned
by the sound of the lash on the backs of the convicts,
and the cries of fear of the Aboriginal people.

But the song was always greater than the singers
and, in small wooden homes and Churches,
it began to spread throughout a vast and dry land.

At last the song came down to me,
sung softly, gently and lovingly by my parents.
Like so many millions of people before me,
I, too, was captivated by the song,
and I wanted to sing and dance it with my whole being.

The song must not stop with our generation,
and we in our turn must hand on its beauty to those who come
after us.
And, as we do so,
we should always remember that this song
has two special characteristics.

The first is that, while we too sing it badly,
nevertheless, as long as we sing to the best of our ability,
others will hear not just our weak voice,
but behind and through us
they will hear a stronger and a surer voice,
the voice of Jesus himself.

The second is that we will always sing it better
whenever we can learn to sing it together
–not one voice here, another there,
singing different words to different melodies–
but all singing together as one.
For then at last the whole world will truly know
that this is still the most beautiful song
the world has ever known.

4

The Divine in Human Hands

At the end of his time on earth Jesus Christ returned to his Father–
and everything began to go downhill from there!!!

Jesus Christ made one terrible mistake:
he brought incredible beauty to earth,
but then, inexplicably, he gave it all into the hands of weak human
beings.
Surely he had to know how great a disorder they would make of it!
Surely anyone could have told him that even his most devoted
followers
would never live up to the ideals he put before them!
The whole sad history of the next two thousand years
was already there in that one catastrophic mistake.
How could someone as intelligent as Jesus
have got things so fundamentally and obviously wrong?

The only answer that can be given
is that God's overwhelming desire for the human race
is that we should grow towards all we are capable of being,
so that we may return the world to the love from which it came.
And God knows that the only way that this can happen
is by our taking responsibility for our own actions
and gradually and painfully learning and growing.
However messy this process and however long it takes,
there is no other way.

If Jesus somehow remained on earth and directed the Church,
people would never grow as they should.
Just as God waited 13.8 billion years for the world
to reach the stage of development it has,
so God can wait for as long as is needed
for the slow development of the Christian Church.

The most essential requirement for proper growth is humility–
the recognition that the example of Jesus is far above us,
and that we have to keep learning.
So the worst fault is that of pride,
particularly in the form of thinking that human beings
have certain answers to every question about Jesus,
so that they now possess him,
can wrap him up in a package
and hand him to others,
for this involves the danger of creating their own religion
rather than being faithful to that of Jesus.

1

When Is Sex Natural?[1]

The thesis of this chapter is in three parts:

1. There is no possibility of a change in the teaching of the Catholic Church on homosexual acts unless and until there is first a change in its teaching on heterosexual acts;

2. There is a serious need for radical change in the Church's teaching on heterosexual acts;

3. If and when this change occurs, it will inevitably have its effect on teaching on homosexual acts.

Part One

There is no possibility of a change in the teaching of the Catholic Church on homosexual acts unless and until there is first a change in its teaching on heterosexual acts.

The constantly repeated argument of the Catholic Church is that God created human sex for two reasons: as the means by which new human life is brought into being (the procreative aspect) and as a means of expressing and fostering love between a couple (the unitive aspect). The argument then says that the use of sex is 'according to

---

1. While the present chapter was first written for a large group of lesbian, gay, bisexual and transgender (LGBT) people, it will be seen that it also applies to wider questions of sexual morality.

nature' only when it serves both of these God-given purposes, and that both are truly present only within marriage, and even then only when intercourse is open to new life, so that all other use of the sexual faculties is morally wrong.[2]

If the starting point is that every single sexual act must be both unitive and procreative, there is no possibility of approval of homosexual acts. The Catechism of the Catholic Church deals with the question with quite extraordinary brevity: '(Homosexual acts) are contrary to the natural law. They close the sexual act to the gift of life. They do not proceed from a genuine affective and sexual complementarity.'[3]

If this is the starting point, there is little else to be said. There is no possibility of change concerning homosexual acts *within* this teaching, and it is futile to look for it, for homosexual acts do not possess the procreative element as the Church understands that element. If teaching on homosexual acts is ever to change, the basic teaching governing all sexual acts must first change.

Part Two

There is a serious need for radical change in the Church's teaching on heterosexual acts.

---

2. The most important papal document on sexual morality of the last century, the encyclical letter *Humanae Vitae,* expressed the argument thus: '*Such teaching, many times set forth by the teaching office of the Church, is founded on the unbreakable connection, which God established and which men and women may not break of their own initiative, between the two meanings of the conjugal act: the unitive meaning and the procreative meaning. Indeed, in its intimate nature, the conjugal act, while it unites the spouses in a most profound bond, also places them in a position (idoneos facit) to generate new life, according to laws inscribed in the very being of man and woman. By protecting both of these essential aspects, the unitive and the procreative, the conjugal act preserves in an integral manner the sense of mutual and true love and its ordering to the exalted vocation of human beings to parenthood.*' Pope Paul VI, encyclical letter *Humanae Vitae,* 26th July 1968, no 12.

3. *Catechism of the Catholic Church,* St Paul's, #2357.

In an ideal world, a man and woman are drawn to each other by love; they marry and have children, and then over many years they help these children to grow to maturity in their physical, intellectual, emotional, social, artistic, moral and spiritual lives, so that they may be ready, in their turn, to found their own families.

In normal circumstances the growth of the union between the parents and the growth to maturity of the children go together, so I have no problem with the idea that marriage and family as institutions of the human race have both a procreative and a unitive aspect.

But to move from this to the idea that every single act of intercourse must contain both the unitive and the procreative aspects is an enormous leap rather than a modest and logical step, and I have five serious difficulties with it.

The First Difficulty: A Sin against God

The first difficulty is that through this teaching the Church is saying that all use of sex that is not both procreative and unitive is a direct offence against God because it is a violation of what is claimed to be the divine and natural order that God established. This raises two serious questions, one concerning nature and the other concerning God.

The question concerning nature
If this divine and natural order exists in relation to our sexual organs, should it not exist in many other areas of human life as well? Should not the Church's arguments concerning sex point to many other fields where God has given a divine purpose to some created thing, such that it would be a sin against God to use that thing in any other way? Why is it that it is only in relation to our sexual organs that this claim is made, and not for any other part of our body or any other human activity?

The question concerning God
Striking a king or president has always been considered a more

serious offence than striking an ordinary citizen. In line with this, it was said, the greatest king by far is God, so an offence against God is far more serious than an offence against a mere human being.

Because all sexual sins were seen as direct offences against God, they were, therefore, all seen as most serious sins. Sexual sins were seen as on the same level as the other sin that is directly against God, blasphemy, and this helps to explain why, in the Catholic Church, sexual morality has long been given a quite exaggerated importance.

For centuries the Church has taught that every sexual sin is a mortal sin.[4] In this field, it was held, there are no venial sins. According to this teaching, even deliberately deriving pleasure from thinking about sex with anyone other than one's spouse, no matter how briefly, is a mortal sin. The teaching may not be proclaimed aloud today as much as before, but it was proclaimed by many popes,[5] it has never been retracted and it has affected countless people.

This teaching fostered belief in an incredibly angry God, for this God would condemn a person to an eternity in hell for a single unrepented moment of deliberate pleasure arising from sexual desire. This idea of God is totally contrary to the entire idea of God that Jesus presented to us, and I cannot accept it.

My first questioning of Church teaching on sex came, therefore, not directly from a rejection of what the Church said about sex, but a rejection of the false god that this teaching presented.

The teaching has also been at the heart of the poor response of the Catholic Church to revelations of sexual abuse. For too many Church leaders it was the sexual act and pleasure involved in abuse that was the great mortal sin, while any harm caused to the minor was lesser, for the sexual sin was a sin against God, while the harm to the minor was merely an offence against a human being.

---

4.   See Noldin-Schmitt, *Summa Theologiae Moralis* (Innsbruck Feliciani Rauch, 1960), Volume I, Supplement *De Castitate*, page 17, no 2; Aertnys-Damen, *Theologia Moralis*, (Rome: Marietti, 1956), volume 1, no 599, 575. The technical term constantly repeated was *mortale ex toto genere suo*. The sin of taking pleasure from thinking about sex was called *delectatio morosa*.

5.   For example, Clement VII (1592–1605) and Paul V (1605–1621) said that those who denied this teaching should be denounced to the Inquisition.

Furthermore, there is a long history of sexual sins being easily forgiven in confession, with the person being then completely restored to the situation before the offence, and this thinking contributed to the moving around of offending priests. Abuse was seen as a sexual sin, and was to be treated like any other sexual sin. Many Church leaders have been very slow to see that this type of thinking is totally wrong and dangerous, for it seriously downplays the harm done to the minor and the indignation of God at this harm. It has created a profound flaw at the heart of the Church's response to abuse.

The Second Difficulty: A Teaching Based on Assertions

The second reason for change is that the statements of the Church appear to be assertions rather than arguments.

Both the unitive and procreative elements are foundational aspects of marriage as an institution of the whole human race, but does it follow:

- that they are essential elements of each individual marriage, no matter what the circumstances?

- that they are essential elements of every single act of sexual intercourse? On what basis?

For example, a particular couple might be told by medical experts that any child they had would suffer from a serious and crippling hereditary illness, and so decide to adopt rather than have children of their own. Are they acting against God's will? Another couple might decide that they already have several children and that they are both financially and psychologically unable to add to their family. On what basis is it claimed that they would be acting against God's will?

There are always problems when human beings claim that they know the mind of God. So is the statement that it is God's will, and indeed order, that both the unitive and procreative aspects must necessarily be present in each act of sexual intercourse a proven fact or a simple assertion? If it is a proven fact, what are the proofs? Why do Church documents not present such proofs?[6] Would not any proofs have to include the experience of millions of people in the very human endeavour of seeking to combine sex, love and the procreation of new life in the midst of the turbulence of human sexuality and the complexities of human life? Is an ideal being confused with a reality?

If it is only an assertion, is there any reason why we should not apply the principle of logic: what is freely asserted may be freely denied? If it is no more than an assertion, does it really matter who it is who makes the assertion or how often it is made? Where are the arguments in favour of the assertion that would convince an open and honest conscience?

The Third Difficulty: A Morality of Physical Acts

The third argument is that the teaching of the Church is based on a consideration of what is seen as the God-given nature of the physical acts in themselves, rather than on these acts as actions of human beings. And it continues to do this at a time when the whole trend in moral theology is in the opposite direction.

As a result it gets into impossible difficulties in analysing physical acts without a context of human relations. For example, some married couples find that there is a blockage preventing the sperm from reaching the ovum, but that in a simple procedure a doctor can take the husband's sperm and insert it into the wife in such a way that it passes the blockage and enables conception. But the Congregation for the Doctrine of the Faith condemned this action because the physical act was not considered 'integral', even though the entire reason for the intervention was precisely that the couple wanted their marriage to be both unitive and procreative.

---

6.   In recent years there has been an appeal to anthropology, but I have not seen a clear statement of how anthropology demands that every act of intercourse include both the unitive and procreative purpose.

The Church's arguments concerning sex are based solely on the physical act in itself rather than on the physical act as an action affecting persons and relationships.

The Fourth Difficulty: The Idea of 'Natural'

It was God who created a world in which there are both heterosexuals and homosexuals. This was not a mistake on God's part that human beings are meant to repair; it is simply an undeniable part of God's creation.

The only sexual acts that are natural to homosexuals are homosexual acts. This is not a free choice they have made between two things that are equally attractive to them, but something that is deeply embedded in their nature, something they cannot simply cast aside. Homosexual acts come naturally to them, heterosexual acts do not. They cannot perform what the Church would call 'natural' acts in a way that is natural to them.

The only exercise of freedom there is for the homosexual is in choosing to move from denial to acceptance and, through this, choosing to be who and what each of them is.

Why should we turn to some abstraction in determining what is natural rather than to the actual lived experience of human beings? Why should we say that homosexuals are acting against nature when they are acting in accordance with the only nature they have ever experienced?

The Church claims that it is basing itself on 'natural law', but a natural law based on abstractions is a false natural law. Indeed, it brings the whole concept of natural law into disrepute.

The Fifth Difficulty: Not Based on the Teaching of Jesus

The fifth difficulty is that the entire idea of the necessity for both the unitive and procreative element in each act of intercourse is not based on anything Jesus said or implied, but comes from ideas outside the bible concerning acts that are said to be natural and acts that are said to be against nature.

Of course philosophical thinking is justified and necessary in relation to sexual morality, as it is in every other field, but for Christians it must always be combined with our study of the scriptures, and this is singularly lacking in relation to sexual morality.

The Dilemma

In the light of these five difficulties, we are left with the fact that the Catholic Church is propounding a teaching that, on logical grounds, has had little appeal to people, even those favourably disposed. Even within the Church, most people no longer accept it, especially among the young. Western society as a whole has rejected this teaching and gone to a position that is in many ways an opposite extreme.

Few people would today attempt a rational defence of the Church's teaching, and it is not easy even to put forward a middle ground between the two extremes. Despite the difficulties, it is this middle ground that I now wish to explore.

The Middle Ground

If we decide to leave behind an ethic that sees sex in terms of a direct, and always mortal, offence against God, that emphasises physical acts rather than persons and relationships, that does not come from the gospels, and that is based on an assertion rather than a logical argument, where should we go?

I suggest that the answer is that we should move to an ethic that:

1. sees any offence against God as being brought about, not by the sexual act in and of itself, but by the harm caused to human beings;

2. speaks in terms of persons and relationships rather than physical acts;

3. draws its ideas of what is natural from experience rather than abstractions;

4. draws consciously and directly on the gospels,

5. and then builds an argument on these foundations rather than on unproven assertions.

From God's point of view
If it is impossible to sustain an entire sexual ethic on the basis of direct offences against God, all the evidence tells us that God cares greatly about human beings and takes a very serious view of any harm done to them, through sexual desire or any other cause.

> *If any of you put a stumbling block before one of these little ones who believe in me, it would be better for you if a great millstone were hung around your neck and you were thrown into the sea.* (Mk 9:42)

> *Then they will answer, 'Lord, when was it that we saw you hungry or thirsty or a stranger or naked or sick or in prison, and did not take care of you?' Then he will answer them, 'Truly I tell you, just as you did not do it to one of the least of these, you did not do it to me'.* (Mt 25:44–45)

In these two quotations Jesus identifies with the weakest persons in the community, and tells us that any harm done to them is a harm done to himself. I suggest that this harm done to people is the real sin in matters of sex, the only sin that angers God.

I suggest, therefore, that we should look at sexual morality in terms of the good or harm done to persons and the relationships between them rather than in terms of a direct offence against God. Following from this, may we say that sexual pleasure, like all other pleasure, is in itself morally neutral, neither good nor bad? Is it rather the circumstances affecting persons and relationships that make this pleasure good or bad, for example, a good pleasure for a married couple seeking reconciliation after a disagreement, a bad pleasure for a man committing rape?

The Church v modern society
To take this further, if we go beneath the particular teachings of the Catholic Church on sex and come to its most foundational beliefs, I suggest that there is a fundamental point on which the Church and modern Western society appear to be moving in opposite directions.

In its simplest terms, the Church is saying that, because love is all-important in human life and because sex is so vital a way of expressing love, sex is serious, while modern society has become more and more accepting of the most casual sexual activity, even when in no way related to love or relationship. For many people sex is in itself 'a bit of fun'.

On this basic point I find myself instinctively more in sympathy with the views of the Church than with those of modern society. Paradoxically, it was the effects of sexual abuse on minors more than anything else that convinced me that all sex is serious.

Do not harm v love your neighbour

Precisely because I see sex as serious, capable of bringing great benefits or causing great damage, I cannot simply conclude that all sex is good as long as it does not harm anyone. I would never want to put the matter in those simple terms, for I have seen far too much harm caused by this attitude.

It is expressed in negative terms ('Do not harm') and inevitably contains within itself the serious risk of brinkmanship, that is, that, with little thought for the good of the other person involved, one may seek one's own pleasure and, in doing so, go right up to the very brink of causing harm to another. In a field as turbulent as this, countless people basing themselves on such a principle will go over that brink.

If we turn to the gospels, Jesus said 'Love your neighbour' rather than 'Do not harm your neighbour', and love implies more than the negative fact of not harming. It implies a genuine respect for the other and positively wanting and seeking the good of the other. The essential difference between the two is that an attitude of 'Do no harm' can put oneself first, while 'Love your neighbour' must put the neighbour first.

In applying this principle of Jesus, we must take the harm that can be caused by sexual desire very seriously, and look carefully at the circumstances that can make morally bad the seeking of sexual pleasure because they involve harm to others, to oneself or to the community. Some of these factors are: violence, physical or psychological, deceit and self-deceit, harming a third person (for example, a spouse), treating people as sexual objects rather than as persons, trivialising sex so that it loses its seriousness, failing to respect the connection that exists between sex and new life, failing to respect the need to build a relationship patiently and carefully, failing to respect the common good of the whole community.

It will be seen from all of this that, even though I see sexual pleasure as in itself morally neutral, I have most serious difficulties with the idea that 'anything goes'. In reacting against one extreme, there is always the danger of going to the opposite extreme. I believe that this is what modern society has done in relation to sex.

A Christian ethic
I suggest that the central questions concerning sexual morality are:

> Are we moving towards a genuinely Christian ethic if we base our sexual actions on a profound respect for persons and for the relationships between them that give meaning, purpose and direction to human life, and on loving our neighbour as we would want our neighbour to love us?

> Within this context, may we ask whether a sexual act is morally right when, positively, it is based on a genuine love of neighbour, that is, a genuine desire for what is good for the other person, rather than solely on self-interest, and, negatively, contains no damaging elements such as harm to a third person, any form of coercion or deceit, or any harm to the ability of sex to express love?

> Is the question of when these circumstances might apply, and whether and to what extent they might apply outside marriage, one for discussion and debate by both the Church community and the wider community, and for decision and responsibility before God, other people and one's own deeper self by each individual?

Many would object that what I have proposed would not give a clear and simple rule to people. But God never promised us that everything in the moral life would be clear and simple. Morality is not just about doing right things; it is also about struggling to know what is the right thing to do. It is not just about doing what everyone else around us is doing; it is about taking a genuine personal responsibility for everything we do. And it is about being profoundly sensitive to the needs and vulnerabilities of the people with whom we interact.

I believe that there is normally a far better chance of a sexual act meeting the requirements I have suggested within a permanent vowed relationship than outside such a relationship. But I could not draw the simple conclusion that: inside a vowed relationship everything is good, outside everything is bad. The complexities of human nature and the turbulence of sexuality do not allow for such simple answers.

The encyclical *Humanae* Vitae of 1968 was a genuine watershed in the relationship between papal teaching and Catholic people, for it was the first time in the history of the Church that the Catholic people as a whole heard a solemn pronouncement of a pope on a matter of faith and morals, paused to relate it to their own experience and knowledge, and then collectively said a firm 'No'. We must not underestimate the permanent importance of this moment. It led to the near universal conviction that popes and bishops can be wrong, especially on sex, so people have to make up their own minds on matters such as pre-marital sex, gay sex, divorce, the ordination of women, and anything else dealing with either sex or gender. The tidal wave of sexual abuse then came in to reinforce these ideas strongly. I cannot see the slightest possibility of the Catholic people as a whole ever returning to the current hierarchical teaching on sexual morality. If the gap between the two is to be bridged, it must be on the basis of mutual acceptance of a middle ground. I hope that I have pointed in fruitful directions.

Part Three

If and when this change (in the teaching concerning heterosexual acts) occurs, it will have its effect on teaching on homosexual acts.

If we apply what I have just said about heterosexual acts to homosexual acts, several things follow.

Negatively, I could not accept for homosexual acts, any more than I can for heterosexual acts, that 'anything goes', or that morality can be based on self-interest or on nothing more than the brinkmanship involved in the idea of 'not harming' another person. I would ask that homosexual persons be as conscious as heterosexual persons of how easily thoughts about sex can be directed solely towards self-interest and lead to harm. I could not applaud a deliberate lifestyle of many transient sexual partners, any more than I could applaud this in heterosexuals, for I cannot see how this could be reconciled with everything I have said in this chapter.

Positively, it would follow that sexual acts, whether heterosexual or homosexual, are not, in and of themselves alone, offensive to God. It would mean that sexual acts are pleasing to God when they help to build persons and relationships, displeasing to God when they harm persons and relationships. Since I seek a specifically Christian ethic, I would always hope that they be based on a genuine loving or willing the good of the other rather than solely on self-interest or self-gratification.

If Church teaching were based on persons and relationships rather than on what is considered 'according to nature' in the physical act, consideration of homosexual acts would exist in a whole new world and would have to be rethought from the very beginning.

In short, if you wish to change the Church's teaching concerning homosexual acts, then work to bring about change in its teaching on all sexual acts.

Scripture

There are statements in the Scriptures that appear to condemn homosexual acts. There are five in particular: two in the First

Testament (Gen 19 and Lev 18:22) and three in the Second (Rom 1:26–27, I Cor 6:9–10, and I Tim 1:9–10). While there are difficulties in interpreting all five, they cannot simply be brushed aside. Despite this, there are four points to keep in mind.

The first is that we must be very careful of language. The First Testament calls homosexuality an abomination, but in that Testament the word 'abomination' is used 138 times and of many different things, for example eating forms of seafood such as prawns (shrimp) that do not have fins and scales.[7] Rather than take the meaning of the word 'abomination' from a modern dictionary, we should see it as a technical word in the law of ancient Israel deriving from ideas concerning what is ritually clean and unclean.

The second factor is that, at the time these parts of the bible were written, there was little of even the limited understanding of homosexuality that we possess today. It seems that it was believed that all persons were in fact heterosexual. Homosexual acts were, therefore, seen as the deliberate choice by heterosexual persons of homosexual actions. Granted the fears that can be aroused in heterosexuals by homosexuality, it is easy to understand why someone such as St Paul could not understand heterosexual persons performing homosexual actions, was thoroughly uncomfortable with the idea, considered these acts 'unnatural' and condemned them. All statements in the Scriptures concerning homosexual actions must be read against this background of a lack of understanding of homosexuality.

The third factor is that, in the culture of ancient Israel, there was a sexual hierarchy in which men were dominant and women submissive. Under this understanding, in a homosexual act a dominant man was treated as a submissive woman, and this was considered wrong.

The fourth factor is that the bible is essentially the story of a journey, the spiritual journey of the people of Israel. As such, it has a beginning, a middle and an end. If Jesus represents the end of

---

7.   'Everything in the waters that has not fins and scales is an abomination to you.' (Lev 11:12)

the journey, we may see its beginning in a person such as Lamech in chapter four of Genesis, who demanded seventy-sevenfold vengeance for any wrong done to him. The bible does not contain only perfect statements of eternal truth, but every stage of this very human journey, including many words and actions that we are definitely not meant to imitate (for example, Jephthah sacrificing his daughter to fulfil a vow in Judg 11:29–40). Statements concerning a subject such as homosexuality must be seen within the context of this journey. For instance, the statement on homosexuality in Leviticus 18:22 comes from a purity ethic that Jesus would later reject, so it cannot be seen as the final word of God on this subject. Indeed, these references need to be relegated to the ethical dustbin along with similar prescriptions for the stoning of women for adultery, etc.

The statements on homosexuality in the Second Testament do not give convincing reasons for their prohibitions, leaving us with the feeling that they are a relic from the purity laws.

Even more, it seems that, when the Church began to treat of sexuality in terms of natural and unnatural acts, the purity ethic of the First Testament heavily influenced its attitude towards homosexual acts.

In short, it is hard to build too great an edifice on these texts.

It remains true that the entire field of sexual morality is in urgent need of being studied again from the foundations up. This will have its effect on teaching on homosexuality, contraception, pre-marital sex, and on sexual morality in general.

2

Divorce and Remarriage

Traditions and the great tradition
My faith is faith in a person and a story: the person of Jesus Christ and the story of his life, death and resurrection. From my response of faith to this person and story flow truths that I believe, moral rules that I follow in trying to be faithful to the example of Christ, a worship that I give to him and a faith community that I belong to. But the person and the story come first. Without that person and story, the truths would be empty, the moral rules would be burdensome tasks, the worship would be lifeless and the faith community would be merely a human institution. With the person and story, the truths come alive, the moral rules become natural ways of acting, the worship is life-giving and the faith community serves some of my deepest needs.

The particular truths that we have been able to discern constitute the 'traditions' (in the plural and with a small 't') that have come down to us. But theologians also speak of the Great Tradition,[1] the essential handing on of the living reality of the person and story of Jesus Christ from one generation to the next, that which I have called 'the Song of Jesus'. Any truths or traditions that we formulate must always be tested against the Great Tradition and must be in conformity with that Tradition.

---

1. The Faith and Order movement of the World Council of Churches, at its meeting in Montreal, 1963, 'distinguished between Tradition and traditions: the former is the "living reality" of revelation that is mediated through all the diversity of the latter.' Paul Avis in the entry on 'Tradition' in *The Oxford Companion to Christian Thought, Intellectual, Spiritual, and Moral Horizons of Christianity,* edited by Adrian Hastings, Alistair Mason and Hugh Pyper (Oxford: Oxford University Press, 2000), 712.

When we study a particular truth, we should always, therefore, look at the scriptural texts in the light of all we have come to know about the *person* of Jesus Christ, the values he constantly held, the priorities he lived and taught, and the manner in which he constantly acted. We must be humble, cautious and diffident in our claims to know and understand him, and yet our collective knowledge of Jesus Christ is surely a tool that we not only may, but must use in our attempts to understand any of the sayings that occur in the gospels. To study a particular text in isolation from the person and story would surely be misguided.

In relation to divorce, it would be all too easy to say that Jesus was supremely loving, so he would have felt compassion for divorced people and have freely admitted divorce. But Jesus could also be supremely challenging; he could tell the Pharisees in the most forthright manner that they were misguided and tell Peter that his thoughts came from Satan. There is more complexity and balance in Jesus than can be summed up in any one sweeping statement. If we are to use this tool of the person of Jesus, we must use it intelligently and carefully. As I hope we shall see, his attitude to divorce was careful and directed at specific targets.

Divorce

The practice of divorce in the Israel in which Jesus lived was very different from that with which we are familiar in our own day, so it would be a serious mistake to think of divorce as practised in Western society today and imagine that this is what the gospels are referring to whenever the word 'divorce' is used. There were two major points of difference.

The first is that the husband alone had the right to divorce. The wife had no appeal and, indeed, few rights of any kind in the matter. The only way in which she herself could secure a divorce was by putting pressure on her husband to divorce her.

The second is that there were no civil courts decreeing divorce, and no legally binding provisions for custody or maintenance. Indeed, there were no obligatory public procedures at all, and the matter was ruled by custom passed down within the tribe, clan or family. The most common requirement was the handing over to the wife by the husband of a certificate of divorce in the presence of two witnesses.

The grounds of divorce were very broad. From very early times ancient Israel was an honour-shame society, that is, one in which the honour of the male in the eyes of the community was of the utmost importance, and anything that was seen as bringing shame on him was treated with great seriousness. So if a man believed that his wife had brought shame on him, for example. by some extramarital sexual action, divorce was seen as obligatory, the only means of restoring his honour.[2]

By the time of Jesus, however, things had developed a long way from this and there were few restrictions on the husband's power to divorce.

Countless commentators have at this point referred to the controversy over the grounds of divorce between the scribal schools of Shammai and Hillell, but John P Meier insists that this controversy belongs to a later time. He quotes many sources to show that at the time of Jesus divorce was an accepted fact of life in Jewish society and the grounds were very broad.[3]

It followed that the position of women in relation to marriage was precarious. And a woman divorced by her husband had no standing in the community and could easily find herself destitute.

We must see the statements of Jesus concerning divorce primarily in relation to this world of first century Israel. Only then can we apply them to our own time.

Adultery

The general understanding of adultery in our own times is that

---

2. In the story told in the gospel of Matthew, Joseph would have stood out from the crowd when, 'being a righteous man and unwilling to expose her to public disgrace, (he) planned to dismiss her quietly' (1:19). For other men the public disgrace of the unfaithful wife would have been seen as an essential part of the restoration of their own good name.

3. See *A Marginal Jew* (New Haven: Yale University Press, 2009), Volume IV, 74–181.

it is voluntary sexual intercourse between a married person and someone other than their spouse. Before we decide, however, that this is the meaning we must give to the term in the gospels, we need to consider two facts.

In the whole of the ancient world, not just in Israel, the basic unit of society was not the individual, but the family, so that a society was primarily seen as a collection of families. In each family the husband was lord and master. His wife or wives were quite literally his property, and adultery was then the violation of this *property right*. If a married woman had intercourse with any man other than her husband, it was always adultery, for it violated the property rights of her husband. If a man had intercourse with a married woman, it was also adultery, for he had violated the property rights of the woman's husband. But if a married man had intercourse with a single woman, it was not adultery, for the property rights of no husband were violated. Thus the term 'adultery' had little to do with the breaking of a promise or with harm to a love relationship, but rather related to the stealing of the 'property' of a male.

The second fact is that in Matthew 5:27–28 Jesus is reported as saying, *'You have heard that it was said, 'You shall not commit adultery.' But I say to you that everyone who looks at a woman with lust has already committed adultery with her in his heart.*

For Jesus sin existed in the mind and heart, and the external action was simply the result of the sin that had already occurred in the mind and heart. Thus, when divorce was contemplated, Jesus saw the adultery as occurring long before the formal divorce and remarriage, and long before any act of sexual intercourse had occurred. Adultery had occurred as soon as a man said to himself, 'I know this woman is married, but I want her and I'm going to do all I can to have her'.

There are five passages from the Second Testament that we must consider, and they may be divided into two pairs and one single text. Matthew 19:1–12 appears to be Matthew's reworking of Mark 10:2–12, so these two texts may be considered together. Matthew 5:31–32 and Luke 16:18 both appear to depend on the same Q source, so they may also be considered together. That leaves the single text, Paul's statement in 1 Corinthians 7:10–15. I shall consider the texts in this order.

The Gospel of Mark

10:2. Some Pharisees came, and to test him they asked, 'Is it lawful for a man to divorce his wife?' The scene is presented as one of confrontation ('to test him'), with the Pharisees seeking ammunition to use against Jesus. For this reason, each of the four verses 3–6 begins with the word 'but', implying a continuing argument between the two sides. The question concerned an issue (the very fact of divorce) where the Pharisees thought they were on certain ground, for I have already noted that in ancient Israel divorce was simply a fact of life, not really queried by anyone. The basic First Testament text on divorce is to be found in Deuteronomy 24:1–4. It simply accepted divorce as a fact of life and added two requirements: the husband had to write out a bill of divorce and give it to his wife before two witnesses, and he could never marry her again once she had married another man. It says much that this text, dealing with the rare case of a man wishing to remarry his first wife after he had divorced her and she had been married to another man, became the standard text on divorce in the First Testament. It was the standard text because there was so little else on the subject. Divorce was a given, a fact of life.

3. (But) He answered them, 'What did Moses command you?' Instead of giving his own view, Jesus followed the constant scribal practice of answering a question with a question, taking the Pharisees back to the basis of their own beliefs in the law of Moses. His choice of the word 'command' was a tactical move, for the direct answer to this question would be that all that Moses had commanded was that, if a man divorced, he must give a written bill of divorce and may never marry the same woman again.

4. (But) They said, 'Moses allowed a man to write a certificate of dismissal and to divorce her.' Instead of saying what Moses *commanded*, the Pharisees spoke of what he had *allowed* and, in doing so, they were tacitly admitting that Moses had not commanded divorce. If divorce occurred, it was the people's, or at least the men's, own choice.

5. **But Jesus said to them, 'Because of your hardness of heart he wrote this commandment for you'.** In the First Testament the term 'hardheartedness' refers to the insensitivity that comes from continual disobedience to God.[4] The force of the verse is that the people had for so long been disobedient that they had lost their sensitivity to God, so that Moses had been able to do no more than salvage what he could by imposing some minimal restrictions.

6. **but from the beginning of creation.** The Pharisees had asked, 'Is it lawful', and by this they meant 'Is it according to the law that came from God through Moses?' In his answer Jesus took the radical step of reinterpreting this law by asking, 'Is the law of Moses on this point a true and full reflection of the mind of God?', and it was this question, not theirs, that he would now answer.[5] *It is crucial to note that the entire argument of Jesus in this passage in Mark's gospel is based on his appeal from a situation created by human insensitivity to the original intention of God.*

God made them male and female. These words are a quotation from Genesis 1:27, stating that from the original intention of God human beings are essentially both male and female, with all their natural attraction and complementarity.

---

4.   The Greek word *sklerokardia* is still used in modern medicine. 'When Jesus affirmed that Moses framed the provision concerning the letter of dismissal out of regard to the people's hardness of heart, he was using an established legal category of actions allowed out of consideration for wickedness or weakness. What is involved is the lesser of two evils . . .' William L Lane, *The New International Commentary on the New Testament, The Gospel of Mark* (Grand Rapids: Erdmans, 1974), 55. ' . . . hardness of heart is a major biblical theme. Since in biblical anthropology the heart is the source of understanding and judgment as well as emotions, hardness of heart involves closing off one's mind and emotions from the truth.' John R Donoghue and Daniel J Harrington, *The Gospel of Mark,* Sacra Pagina Series (Collegeville: Liturgical Press, 2002), 293.

5.   'The error of the Pharisees lay in their losing sight of this distinction (between an absolute divine command and a divine provision to deal with situations brought about by men's "hardness of heart") and so imagining that Deut 24:1 meant that God allowed divorce, in the sense that it had his approval and did not come under his judgment.' Augustine Stock OSB, *The Method and Message of Mark* (Wilmington: Michael Glazier, 1989), 265.

7. **For this reason a man shall leave his father and mother and be joined to his wife, and the two shall become one flesh.** This verse also contains a quotation from Genesis, but this time from the earlier account of creation in the second chapter of Genesis (2:24), the story of Adam and Eve. In this account all the animals were brought to the man and he gave each one its name (2:19–20), implying, in Jewish understanding, that he both understood their nature and had power over them. Precisely for these reasons, however, the animals did not satisfy him (2:20b). So God said that he would provide a helper for the man, and the word used, *ezer,* does not imply a subservient helper, for in the First Testament it is used also of God as our mighty helper. God then brought the woman to him and this time he could not give her a new name, but only his own name (*ish*) with a feminine ending (*ishshah*). The words 'For this reason . . .' follow immediately, implying that the man did find true satisfaction in the woman and that this happened precisely because he could not name her, for she was his equal.[6] In the mind of Jesus, this was the original divine plan of marriage, and it was only in the security of this plan that marriage could fulfil its role in coming to terms with the restlessness of the human condition (Gen 2:18) and bringing a lasting happiness to people.[7]

8. **so that they are no longer two but one flesh.** These words have their mystery, but would seem to include a number of elements: the unity of flesh in sexual intercourse, the couple becoming as one before both the law and the community, their mutual love and common journey towards God, the two becoming one in their child, and the idea that marriage is such that part of the very being of each married person is the relationship to the other, so that to exclude this relationship is to deny part of one's own being.

---

6. I have taken this interpretation from the book *The Promise to Love* of Wilfrid J Harrington OP (London: Geoffrey Chapman, 1968). Harrington notes that the *ish-ishah* etymology is popular only, not exact. He calls it a typical Hebrew word play. He suggests that it is what the writer intended and helps to make sense of the passage.
7. It is 'an appeal over against legislation based upon fallen history to the true nature of human existence as it was revealed from the beginning of the creation.' William L Lane, *The New International Commentary,* 355–356.

9. Therefore what God has joined together, let no one separate.[8]
The first meaning of these words is that they are a strong rejection of
the universal idea of the times that men were the lords of marriage
and freely decided its terms. They are a statement that for Jesus the
true lord of marriage is God, for in such matters husband as well as
wife must first obey God's will and seek to respect God's original
intentions in establishing marriage.[9]

10. Then in the house the disciples asked (*were asking*) **him again
about this matter.** The questions of the disciples were not polemic,
but came from a genuine desire to understand, so in his reply Jesus
did not seek to confront them as he had the Pharisees. At the same
time, the imperfect tense of 'were asking' implies that the disciples
were slow to accept the answer given them by Jesus and kept asking
their questions.

**11. He said to them, 'Whoever divorces his wife and marries
another commits adultery against her'.** The last two words ('against
her') are of great importance, for by his use of these words Jesus was
proclaiming that the violation of the rights of a wife was also and
equally adultery. This was a truly revolutionary idea, for it meant
that for Jesus a wife had such rights and was, therefore, not the mere
'property' of her husband. This overturned the entire basis on which
the family, and hence the whole of society, had been built. In its
social impact it is arguably the most revolutionary statement in the
gospels, for it demanded a completely new ordering of the whole of
society. It is small wonder that the disciples were slow to grasp the
vast implications of what Jesus was saying.

Marriage can be either a relationship of power and authority
between unequal partners or a love relationship between equal

---

8.   There is a problem in translation here in that the Greek word *anthropos* means a
      human being of either gender, and English has no exact equivalent. The older exclusive
      language at least got the theological point right: 'What *God* has joined, *man* must not
      separate', for it established a clear God-man contrast, implying that God, not human
      beings, set the terms of marriage.

9.   'The Mosaic provision in Deut 24:1–4 was in reality a witness to the gross evil which
      arose from, or even consisted in, a disregard of the creation ordinance of marriage as
      set forth in Gen1:27; 2.24.' Lane, *The New International Commentary*, 355.

partners, but it cannot be both, and it cannot move backwards and forwards between the two at different times. The rights acquired in a wedding ceremony are either rights to property and ownership by the husband, or they are mutual rights to such things as justice, caring, respect and love, but they cannot be both. If they are rights to property, then the marriage contract is really between the father of the bride and the husband. It is a contract in which the father gives his property rights over his daughter to her husband, and she is simply the property or object that is passed over. It is only in a love relationship that the woman has something to give to her husband, so it is only in this case that the marriage is a true contract between the two of them. Furthermore, even if love is the basis on which a couple first enter a marriage, the fact that in Jewish law the man had dominance over the woman and could resort to power at any time placed severe strains on the love relationship. In Jewish law the authority of the husband was always there, and the wife's position was very weak.

12. '**And if she divorces her husband and marries another, she commits adultery.**' It was Roman law that first gave to a wife the right to repudiate her husband, and commentators[10] see this verse as a conclusion drawn by the Christian community from the words of Jesus rather than as a saying that came directly from Jesus himself.[11]

Conclusions from the Text of Mark

I maintain that in this passage Jesus was concerned to do far more than make some changes to divorce practice. He wanted to do away with the entire *system* of both marriage and divorce then in practice and with the attitudes that went behind the system. I believe that any interpretation that has him doing less than this fails to see the full force of the passage.

---

10. L William Countryman, *Dirt, Greed and Sex, Sexual Ethics in the New Testament and Their Implications for Today* (Philadelphia: Fortress Press, 1988), 168–169.
11. This verse in effect has the Church saying to women under Roman law, 'Don't start getting legalistic and claiming that what Jesus said doesn't apply to you because, against his Jewish background, he spoke only of men. It applies to you too.'

Jesus was confronted with a situation where the males in the community were collectively the lords of marriage as a social institution and each man was then lord of his own marriage, with a broad power to divorce his wife. Women were mere property and had no say in the matter. Jesus rebelled against these attitudes, asserting that they came from 'hardness of heart' and that they had not been the original intention of God. He insisted that it is God who is the sole lord of marriage, so all people, male and female, must seek to be true to those things that are inherent in marriage as God created it.

At this point I suggest that two interpretations of the words of this scene are possible. The first is that Jesus was declaring on divine authority that God in the beginning had decreed that marriage is essentially permanent, so no human being may dissolve a marriage. If anyone attempts to do so, the bond created by God remains and any new marriage is not a marriage at all, but adultery. This might seem to be the logical conclusion from the *words*, 'Whoever divorces his wife and marries another commits adultery against her.'

The second possible interpretation is that God in the beginning created human beings male and female, and created them in such a manner that their greatest happiness and growth, their best chance of learning to live creatively with the restlessness of the human condition, are to be found in committing themselves unreservedly and as equals to a lasting union in accordance with a divine plan, and in then doing everything in their power to make sure that the union in fact flourishes and lasts. Each of the couple, therefore, has a powerful *moral* obligation towards the other. This would seem to be the most obvious and literal interpretation of the *argument* Jesus uses.

In presenting this argument, Jesus first issued the challenge that his followers were to do all in their power to regain the creation, the original plan of God, in relation to marriage. He said that the turning away from this plan, by individuals or by whole societies, came from 'hardheartedness'. He then quoted two passages from Genesis concerning God's original intention. The first said that God created human beings male and female, with all their natural attraction and complementarity. The second said that the man and the woman became one flesh precisely because they could find a happiness, fulfilment and satisfaction in each other that creatures such as animals could never provide. Arguing on this basis, he then attacked powerful vested interests of his time, and indeed overturned the entire basis on which society was built, by the quite revolutionary saying that a man could commit adultery against his wife. The second interpretation appears to be the more logical conclusion from this argument.

It seems to me that, in interpreting the meaning of the words, 'Whoever divorces his wife and marries another, commits adultery against her', we must necessarily decide where we are placing the accent and what words we are assuming behind the text. There is a great difference between these two statements: 'Whoever, no matter what the circumstances, divorces his wife and marries another, commits adultery because God has created a bond between them that neither can dissolve', and 'Whoever, for personal benefit and without concern for what happens to his wife, divorces his wife and marries another, leaving the wife open to discrimination and destitution, commits adultery against her'. I suggest that the second saying is closer to the intention of Jesus in this scene.

It also seems to cohere more closely with all we know about the *person* of Jesus from the whole of the gospels. We know that Jesus recognised rights in women that the society around him did not and there are many scenes in which he himself showed a profound respect for their dignity. The power of men over divorce, the idea of a wife as property, the weak position of women in relation to marriage and the destitution of many divorced women constituted a *system* that Jesus found abhorrent, for it was contrary to his deep concern for justice and love.

Furthermore, this *system,* based on a relationship of dominance-subservience, created across the whole of society a form of marriage that would not and could not fulfil the deeper needs for which marriage had been created by God 'in the beginning'. Jesus could not accept this system and he would not make only slight changes to it.

In other words, what Jesus could not agree with in this scene in Mark was a *system* that he saw as an *adulterous system*, understanding the word 'adulterous' in the sense I have already indicated. For men to consider themselves lords of their marriage and free to divorce and remarry as it suited them, without any consideration for their wife, was, in the mind of Jesus, to be already deeply immersed in an adulterous mindset. In accordance with everything we know about him as a *person*, Jesus strongly attacked this system and replaced it with both an insistence on unheard-of rights in the woman and the profoundly challenging ideal of regaining the creation.

The argument that Jesus was saying that, when a couple marry, God specifically intervenes to create a bond that neither can then break does not arise from the arguments used in this scene and it is impossible to find any parallel to it in the gospels. What is this 'bond' that God creates and what basis is there for stating that it exists? In other words, it is not easy to reconcile this idea with the *person* of Jesus as we know him from the rest of the gospels.

In addition, if this is a law enacted on the authority of Jesus, then the *argument* given by Jesus becomes irrelevant. If this is a law about a divine bond, the whole argument stops right there, and whether a man can commit adultery against his wife or whether there were problems in the *system* of marriage and divorce in place at the time become irrelevant. On this understanding, Jesus would have left all those problems in place and done nothing to confront them.

I suggest, therefore, that what Jesus was speaking about here was what God had 'from the beginning of creation' intended marriage to be, including the essential and equal dignity of women, and about some of the powerful and compelling *moral* consequences that flow from this.

> *Jesus was not interested in matrimonial laws, but in rigorous moral teachings like those we may encounter in the Sermon on the Mount.*[12]

---

12. Joachim Gnilka, *Marco* (Assisi: Editrice Citadella, 1987), 534. The translation from the Italian is my own.

I suggest that we shall see that the other texts in the Second Testament support these conclusions.

Matthew 19:1–12

> *Some Pharisees came to him, and to test him they asked, 'Is it lawful for a man to divorce his wife for any cause?' He answered, 'Have you not read that the one who made them at the beginning made them male and female, and said, "For this reason a man shall leave his father and mother and be joined to his wife, and the two shall become one flesh"? So they are no longer two, but one flesh. Therefore what God has joined together, let no one separate.' They said to him, 'Why then did Moses command us to give a certificate of dismissal and to divorce her?' He said to them, 'It was because you were so hard-hearted that Moses allowed you to divorce your wives, but from the beginning it was not so. And I say to you, whoever divorces his wife, except for unchastity, and marries another, commits adultery'. (19:1–10)*

Though there are differences,[13] there are also obvious similarities between this scene and the one in Mark we have already considered. Indeed, this scene is usually accepted as little more than Matthew's reworking of Mark's scene according to his own criteria. In Mark the question had concerned the lawfulness of divorce as such, while in Matthew the question appears to assume the lawfulness of divorce and raises a question concerning the grounds ('for any cause').

In calling back immediately to the intention of God in the creation, Matthew presents Jesus as claiming the moral high ground from the beginning of the discussion and forcing his opponents to prove their case. They introduce the law of Moses, but they go further than is lawful, for they use the word 'command' to cover both the written document of dismissal and the very right to divorce, and we have

---

13. 'Matthew has restructured the argument so that the positive argument about God's will for men and women from the creation comes first and the concession made by Moses comes second.' Harrington, *The Promise to Love*, 274–275.

already seen that, while Moses commanded the written document of dismissal, he did not command divorce. Jesus corrects them in his second answer, saying that Moses allowed, not commanded, divorce, and did so only because of their hard-heartedness. For a second time he calls back to 'the beginning', that is, the original intention of God in the creation. His conclusion is the same as in Mark, 'Whoever divorces his wife and marries another, commits adultery'. Though the words 'against her' are not stated explicitly, they are implicit, for adultery has to be committed against someone, and it is clearly the wife who is intended. Once again, the statement that a man could commit adultery against his wife was startling, radical and revolutionary in its implications.

The conclusions that I drew from the gospel of Mark can be drawn from this passage in Matthew also, for it contains the same essential argument: a call back from the current *system* of marriage and divorce to God's original intention in creating marriage, a quotation concerning the complementarity of man and woman, a quotation from the text stating that only in each other would they find a fulfilment that the animals could never give, and a conclusion that the man could commit adultery, as Jesus understood the term, against his wife. Equally with Mark, it is the condemnation of a *system* of marriage and divorce that all too easily involved an adulterous mindset and harmed the very purposes for which marriage had been created 'in the beginning'.

Except for unchastity

In this passage we must also consider the extra phrase introduced both here and in the passage in Matthew that I shall consider next: 'except in the case of *porneia*'. The word *porneia* can cover any form of sexual impropriety and is better translated by the broad word 'unchastity'.

In understanding this phrase I believe that it is important that we not see Jesus as doing no more than agreeing with those (a fairly small minority) who believed that divorce was permitted only in the case of adultery by the wife, for then his taking the high ground by twice calling back to the will of God in the creation would be meaningless. His reply would no longer be radical or revolutionary,[14] and it would still include the idea that only men could initiate divorce and that women had no rights in the matter. In other words, Jesus would still be approving the *system* of marriage and divorce then in practice. It seems to me that the very essence of this scene is that Jesus was asked to decide between two schools of thought and gave an answer that was more radical than either. I believe that we are on far firmer ground if we see Matthew as being fully as radical as Mark, and this essentially demanded a rejection of the entire *system* of marriage and divorce then in practice.

> *That Jesus was demanding a fidelity to marriage and a commitment to pledged love that went beyond the expectations of his contemporaries of whatever school of thought is obvious from the reaction of his disciples.*[15]

The male disciples (10–12) correctly saw in the words of Jesus the taking away of traditional male rights in this matter:

> *His disciples said to him, 'If such is the case of a man with his wife, it is better not to marry.' But he said to them, 'Not everyone can accept this teaching, but only those to whom it is given. For there are eunuchs who have been so since birth, and there are eunuchs who have been made eunuchs by others, and there are eunuchs who have made themselves eunuchs for the sake of the kingdom of heaven. Let anyone accept this who can.'*[16]

---

14. 'The addition (of the exceptive clause) not only softens the ethics of the kingdom, but it also stands in tension with the absolutism of v 6, weakens the argument of vv 7–8, and makes the disciples' comments in v 10 and Jesus' statements in vv 11–12 less appropriate than would be the case of an absolute prohibition of divorce.' Donald A Hagner, *Matthew 1–13*, Word Biblical Commentary (Dallas: Word Books Publishers, 1993), 549.
15. Michael Fallon MSC, *The Gospel according to Saint Matthew* (Sydney: Chevalier Press, 1997), 261.
16. 'The disciples speak as if the attraction of marriage depended on easy divorce,

There is an immense body of literature on the meaning of the exceptive clause, and most explanations can be reduced to two. Common to both is that the words do not come from Jesus himself, but were added by the early Church.

> *If the Matthean exceptive clause had been a part of the original form of the prohibition, it is extremely difficult to understand how and why Paul, Mark and Luke would all have come up with absolute forms of the prohibition.*[17]

The first explanation is that the words are a true exception. One version (among many) of this is that it is possible that Jewish followers of Jesus might have accepted his ideal of returning to God's original intentions in creating marriage, and even accepted that women had rights, and (with great difficulty under the strong influence of the powerful personality of Jesus) that they even had equal dignity and rights. But, with a lifetime of a culture of honour-shame behind them, they simply could not bring themselves to accept that a man should remain with a wife guilty of adultery or some other serious sexual impropriety. That was altogether too much and the weight of their cultural heritage was too powerful. In this interpretation the early Church, through Matthew, is allowing for this attitude.

This interpretation presupposes that Matthew realised that the words of Jesus had been a statement of powerful moral obligation, to which there can in serious circumstances be exceptions, rather than a divine law about an unbreakable bond, to which there can be no exceptions.

The other explanation of the exceptive clause is that it refers to a marriage within the forbidden degrees of kinship laid down in the First Testament. These laws went beyond those of most other nations, so it was always possible that Christian converts from paganism might already be in a marriage that was forbidden by Jewish law, and hence that would scandalise Jewish converts. The

---

Harrington, *The Promise to Love*, 274.

17.   John P Meier, *A Marginal Jew*, volume IV, 104.

Jews considered such a marriage to be a *porneia*, an unchastity, and believed that in these circumstances divorce was not divorce at all, but the putting aside of a wife whom one should not have married in the first place. The exceptive clause would then have been an addition by the early Church to cover situations that had arisen and were causing scandal to Jewish converts. Chapter 15 of the Acts of the Apostles tells the story of the First Council of Jerusalem, when the early Church introduced laws precisely in order to avoid scandal to Jewish converts. There are, however, some serious problems with this interpretation,[18] and I personally favour the first explanation.

I am unable to take the matter further in terms of analysis of the texts. In accordance with the overriding idea of this article, therefore, I turn to the *person* of Jesus and all we know about his values and how he acted. When the texts are seen in this light, I repeat that I believe it is important that we not adopt an interpretation that would have Jesus doing no more than agreeing with one school of thought, while leaving the *system* of marriage and divorce in place. I suggest that our minimum conclusion must be to assume that there is no contradiction between this scene, the earlier scene in this same gospel that I shall consider next, and the scene in Mark. I suggest that we must see Matthew as being as radical as Mark and, like Mark, both speaking the language of moral obligation rather than of law and rejecting the entire current *system* of marriage and divorce.

Matthew 5:31–32

We now come to the second pair of texts, both seeming to derive from the same statement in the common Q source.

---

18. '1) The context does not indicate at all that Matthew wants to take *porneia* in such a narrow sense and to refer his exception only to the former Gentiles. 2) Correspondingly, no single Church father and no single interpreter up until the modern time would have understood what he was truly concerned about. 3) In Leviticus 18 the word *porneia* is missing. 4) *Parektos logou porneias* is a clear reference to Dt 24:1, but then it must deal with the reasons for the divorce of legitimate and not with the invalidity of illegitimate marriages.' Ulrich Luz, *Matthew 1-7, A Commentary* (Minneapolis: Augsburg Fortress, 1989), 304–305.

> *It was also said, 'Whoever divorces his wife, let him give*
> *her a certificate of divorce.' But I say to you that anyone*
> *who divorces his wife, except on the ground of unchastity,*
> *causes her to commit adultery; and whoever marries a*
> *divorced woman commits adultery.* (5:31–32)

I have already considered the meaning of the words 'except on the ground of unchastity' and shall make no further comment here.

The context of the saying being considered here is that of the Sermon on the Mount (5:1–7:29) and, in particular, the section contained in 5:17–48. It begins by saying,

> *Do not think that I have come to abolish the law or the*
> *prophets; I have not come to abolish but to fulfil.*[19]

Over the following twenty-eight verses (21–48) Jesus then spells out what he means by 'not abolish but fulfil'[20] in a series of sayings in the form, 'You have heard that it was said . . . but I say to you . . .'

> *You have heard that it was said to those of ancient times,*
> *'You shall not murder' . . . But I say to you that if you are*
> *angry with a brother or sister . . . (21–26) . . . 'You shall*
> *not commit adultery'. But I say to you that everyone who*
> *looks at a woman with lust. . . .' (27–30) . . . It was said,*
> *'whoever divorces his wife... but I say to you . . . (31–32)*
> *. . . 'you shall not swear falsely'. . . . But I say to you, 'Do*

---

19. 'The ethical teaching of Jesus that follows in this sermon . . . has such a radical character and goes so much against what was the commonly accepted understanding of the commands of the Torah that it is necessary at the outset to vindicate Jesus' full and unswerving loyalty to the law.' Hagner, *Matthew 1–13*, 103. 'These were the words of a strict Jewish Christian community seeking to maintain absolute obedience to the letter of the Law, probably in opposition to a more liberal interpretation such as those represented by Stephen (cf Acts 7:48ff, 8:1) and later by Paul (Gal 2:2–6, 11:6; Acts 15). Edward Schweizer, *The Gospel according to Matthew* (London: SPCK, 1975), 104.

20. 'When considered in itself, the opposition of 5:17 allows us to say that "to fulfil" is contrasted with "to abolish", that is, to dismantle, tear down, and thus make invalid, annul . . . Fulfilling means, therefore, having a constructive attitude towards Scripture and considering it important, not null.' Daniel Patte, *The Gospel according to Matthew* (Philadelphia: Fortress Press, 1987), 72.

> *not swear at all . . .' (33–37) . . . 'An eye for an eye and a
> tooth for a tooth.' But I say to you . . . 'if anyone strikes
> you on the right cheek, turn the other also . . .' (38–42) . .
> . 'You shall love your neighbour and hate your enemy.' But
> I say to you, 'Love your enemies (43–47) . . . Be perfect,
> therefore, as your heavenly Father is perfect'. (48)*

Though most commentators call these sayings 'antitheses', the word

> *fits the rhetorical pattern but not the content. In some
> cases Jesus expresses agreement with the biblical teaching
> but urges his followers to go deeper or to the root of
> the commandment (murder>anger, adultery>lust,
> retaliation>non-resistance). In other cases Jesus' teaching
> can seem to go so far as to make the biblical commandment
> useless (divorce, oaths, love of neighbour.)[21]*

Furthermore, the sayings concern different orders of law from the
Torah: while the first two concern the Ten Commandments, the
others do not and, indeed, there was no law forbidding divorce itself.

The first thing that appears to be clear is that, while Jesus is
quoting laws from the First Testament, he is not simply replacing
them with new laws. He is leaving the laws in place ('not abolish')
and then expressing moral principles that show the more perfect
way to observe the value that is behind the law ('but fulfil'). To be
perfect as the heavenly Father is perfect or to turn the other cheek
are not new laws. We are not morally deficient if we fail to be as
perfect as the heavenly Father and we are not breaking a law if we
swear an oath in court or fail to turn the other cheek and allow
someone to strike us a second time.

> *Interpreters of these verses must be careful not to translate
> into legal statute what is presented as an evangelic
> counsel. That is, it ought not to be treated differently than*

---

21. Daniel J Harrington SJ, *The Gospel of Matthew*, Sacra Pagina Series (Collegeville: The Liturgical Press, 1991), 90.

the other antitheses, none of which has been or can be converted into law.[22]

The new sayings of Jesus go beyond the external action demanded by the law to moral principles concerning the internal attitudes that lead to the breaking of the law.[23] In this they may be called prescriptive ideals, that is, they are ideals, not laws, but they are prescriptive, for we are meant, and indeed obliged, to strive after them. I do not commit sin if I fail to have warm feelings for my enemies, but I do fail as a follower of Jesus if I do not even see loving my enemies as an ideal that calls to me with genuine power and urgency. I do not fail morally if I am not as perfect as the heavenly Father, but I do fail as a Christian if I do not see being as perfect as the heavenly Father as a goal that might guide my life.

Furthermore, the language of this section needs to be taken into account, for it is Semitic language and so is concrete rather than abstract and involves what our modern Western minds would consider serious exaggeration or overstatement, even extravagance. It is a language that appears to be typical of the *person* of Jesus, for example:

> *If any of you put a stumbling block before one of these little ones who believe in me, it would be better for you if a great millstone were hung around your neck and you were thrown into the sea.* (Mk 9:42)

> *It is easier for a camel to go through the eye of a needle than for someone who is rich to enter the kingdom of God.* (Mk 10:25)

> *Why do you see the speck in your neighbour's eye, but do not notice the log in your own eye?* (Mat 7:3)

---

22. Douglas RA Hare, *Matthew* (Louisville: John Knox Press,1993), 54.

23. 'Common to most is the sense that righteous behaviour has to do with the heart and with attitude rather than with mere conformity with external prescription.' Brendan Byrne, *Lifting the Burden, Reading Matthew's Gospel in the Church Today*, (Sydney: St Paul's Publications, 2004), 58.

So therefore, none of you can become my disciple if you do not give up all your possessions. (Lk 14:33)

It is easier for heaven and earth to pass away, than for one stroke of a letter in the law to be dropped. (Lk 16:17)

Whoever comes to me and does not hate father and mother, wife and children, brothers and sisters, yes, and even life itself, cannot be my disciple. (Lk 14:26)

It is obvious that these sayings should not be understood in a slavishly literal manner.

This type of language abounds in the context of the series of prescriptive ideals that surround this saying on divorce. There we are told by Jesus not to be angry, though in fact we have no direct control over our feelings and cannot prevent feelings of anger whenever a serious wrong is done to us. We are told that if we say to someone, 'You fool', we 'will be liable to the hell of fire', though no one would take this literally. We are told not to look at a woman with lust, though the very continuance of the human race demands that there be sexual desire. We are told that, if our eye causes us to sin, we should tear it out and throw it away, and no Church has ever suggested that we should take these words literally. We are told that we should never swear oaths, and yet both Church and State routinely administer oaths. We are told to turn the other cheek, to give a cloak as well as a tunic and to walk a second mile, though no one interprets these as literal obligations. We are told to love our enemies, though once again we have no direct control over our feelings. Finally, we are told to be perfect as the heavenly Father is perfect, though this is manifestly impossible and we will never come even remotely close to living up to this ideal.

The saying on divorce comes in the middle of these prescriptive ideals (31–32) and this context cannot be ignored. It would surely be nonsense to say that the statements surrounding this one are all prescriptive ideals, not laws, but that the one on divorce is a strict law rather than a prescriptive ideal. It would be nonsense to say that all the surrounding statements use exaggerated Semitic language, but this one uses only literal language. It follows that the saying on divorce must also be seen as a prescriptive ideal rather than as a law. The message must surely be that people are not necessarily committing sin if they divorce, for there may be cases where it is justified, but they are failing if they do not see permanency as a powerful and binding ideal, something that they must strive for with all their might.

These considerations strongly reinforce the idea that the words contained in Mark 10 and Matthew 19 are forceful statements of moral obligation rather than statements of law.

Matthew goes further than Mark, for Mark had spoken only of the case where the man had divorced his wife and married another. Matthew takes two other cases. In the first he has Jesus saying that, if a man divorces his wife, he is causing the wife to commit adultery, presumably by marrying another man. In the second case, he imagines a man marrying a woman who has been divorced, and speaks of this as adultery on his part. Mark had placed the accent on the act of divorcing a wife, while Matthew looks to the remarriage after the divorce, not by the man who divorced his wife, but by the woman who is divorced and by the man marrying her.

The two statements in Matthew 5:32 sound harsher than those of Mark, for they might seem to include the woman divorced by her husband and left destitute, but we must keep firmly in mind the fact that in Matthew they are presented as prescriptive ideals. It follows that Jesus is not saying that either the wife or the second man is necessarily committing sin through a second marriage. What, then, is the prescriptive ideal he is pointing to? I shall return to these questions later in this chapter .

The Gospel of Luke

> *Anyone who divorces his wife and marries another commits adultery, and whoever marries a woman divorced from her husband commits adultery.* (16:18)

This saying is in language very similar to Matthew 5:31–32, so that most scholars believe that both texts come from the Q document that lies behind much of Matthew and Luke.

As it stands in the gospel of Luke, the saying has its difficulties, for the context does nothing to assist us. Beginning in chapter 15 we have a series of parables (the lost sheep, the lost drachma, the prodigal son and the dishonest steward); then we have four sayings that do not appear to have any direct connection either to the parables or to each other, and then we have another parable (the rich man and Lazarus).

The saying on divorce is the fourth of the sayings in the middle of these parables. The first saying may be seen as connected to the parable of the unjust steward immediately preceding it, for it speaks of love of money. But the second deals with the kingdom taking the place of the law and the prophets, and the third with the fact that no detail of the law will be abolished.[24] The third then deals with divorce.[25] So far as can be seen, this saying stands on its own without any particular context.[26]

This lack of context creates problems for an interpreter. There is, however, no reason to think that the gospel of Luke wishes

---

24. 'The second set of sayings in this Lucan editorial unit preceding the parable of the rich man and Lazarus has almost nothing to do with material possessions or ambitious esteem before other human beings, topics of Jesus' comments in vv 1–15.' Joseph A Fitzmyer, *The Gospel According to Luke*, Anchor Bible, (New York: Doubleday and Co, 1985), Volume 2, 1114.

25. 'The third saying in this editorial unit seems to move to an entirely different topic- even less related to the general theme of ch.16 than the sayings on the law in the two preceding verses-*viz* the prohibition of divorce (v16).' Joseph A Fitzmyer, *The Gospel According to Luke*, 1119.

26. In the commentaries I have studied there are many attempts to give a unity to these sayings, but no two seem to agree. Brendan Byrne expresses a common opinion when he says, 'It is hard to account for the series of sayings lying between the two parables in this chapter. The sayings seem disconnected, both with the wider context and among each other.' *The Hospitality of God, A Reading of Luke's Gospel* (Sydney: St Paul's Publications, 2002), 134. Furthermore, the middle two sayings are not at all clear in themselves and there is much debate over their meaning. Commentaries that are most helpful in understanding other parts of Luke's gospel seem to be at something of a loss here. See, for example, Luke Timothy Johnson, *The Gospel of Luke*, Sacra Pagina Series (Collegeville: The Liturgical Press, 1991), 250–251 and 254–255.

to contradict the gospels of Mark or Matthew. Good practice in biblical interpretation would rather say that we should interpret the brief statement without a context in Luke in the light of the longer statements with context given in both Mark and Matthew. We may conclude that Luke is also speaking the language of moral obligation in justice and love rather than law. To dismiss a wife because a man has met another woman he prefers and to leave his wife and the children of the marriage without a man in a world that was built on families was a violation of both justice and love and, therefore, in the eyes of Jesus, adultery. If to the words of Luke we add all the same author says about the *person* of Jesus, we must once again see Jesus insisting, with all the force at his command, on the rights and dignity of the woman and on the moral obligations that flowed from this.

In common with the first saying on divorce in Matthew (5:31–32), Luke also has Jesus speaking of the man who marries a divorced woman. Once again I shall leave comment on this point until after we have looked at the statement of Paul.

The First Letter to the Corinthians 7:10–15

> *To the married I give this command—not I but the Lord—that the wife should not separate from her husband, but if she does separate, let her remain unmarried or else be reconciled to her husband, and that the husband should not divorce his wife.*
> *To the rest I say—I and not the Lord—that if any believer has a wife who is an unbeliever and she consents to live with him, he should not divorce her. And if any woman has a husband who is an unbeliever, and he consents to live with her, she should not divorce him . . .*
> *But if the unbelieving partner separates, let it be so; in such a case the brother or sister is not bound. It is to peace that God has called you . . .*

This letter of Paul to the Corinthians was written around the year 54–55 CE, some fifteen years before any of the gospels, so it is the first testimony to the teaching of Jesus on the subject of divorce.

Paul introduces the topic by saying that he is answering some questions that the Christian community in the city of Corinth had referred to him ('Now concerning the matters about which you wrote ...' 7:1).[27] What follows has been described as similar to listening to one end of a telephone conversation,[28] and Paul had no idea that his simple reply to a letter would one day be considered part of the New Testament and analysed in minute detail. We would love to know the exact questions he was asked, but there is considerable difficulty in determining this.[29]

This creates a problem when we come to the question of divorce. In vv 10 and 12 Paul appears to create an antithesis: 'To the married I give this command—not I but the Lord—... To the rest I say—I and not the Lord'. But who are 'the rest'? They are not 'the unmarried', for this would not make sense of the text. It is possible that 'the married' means those in a marriage of two Christians, while 'the rest' indicates Christians in a mixed marriage with a non-Christian, but this is far from certain.

It appears that the particular case referred to Paul concerns the situation of a Christian whose non-Christian spouse has left and sought a divorce. In his answer, it appears that Paul first quotes his understanding of what Jesus had said ('not I but the Lord'), and then gives his own application of this teaching to the particular case that the community had referred to him ('I and not the Lord').

In presenting his understanding of what Jesus had said, Paul is close to what the gospels will later say. He is unusual in speaking first of the wife leaving her husband, and this implies a practice of divorce different from that of the Jewish world in which Jesus had spoken. It reflects the fact that he was writing to Christians in

27. 'The matters which they raised can be gathered in part from Paul's introducing them with "now concerning"; by this criterion they included: marriage and divorce (7:1), virginity (7:25), food offered to idols (8:1), spiritual gifts (12:1), the collection for Jerusalem (16:1), and Apollos (16:12)'. *1 and 2 Corinthians*, edited by FF Bruce, New Century Bible (London: Oliphants, 1971), 66.

28. 'Paul was asked some definite questions, and he answered them; he was not concerned with developing a full theology of the subject'. Dennis Murphy msc, *The Apostle of Corinth* (Melbourne: Campion Press, 1966), 166.

29. It is most probable that he is quoting or at least summarising the first question when he says in 7:1: 'It is well for a man not to touch a woman'.

the Greek city of Corinth who had been influenced by Greek and Roman practices of divorce. It is also possible, of course, that this was the particular case that had been referred to him.

In applying this teaching of Jesus to the case presented to him, there is no scriptural basis on which to claim that Paul understands himself to be quoting a law laid down by Jesus and then, by virtue of some claim of delegated divine authority, either changing that law or dispensing from it (the so-called 'Pauline Privilege'). It surely makes more sense to say that Paul is quoting the serious moral obligation, the prescriptive ideal, of which Jesus had spoken in relation to marriage and divorce ('not I but the Lord') and is then applying that moral obligation to a particular situation that had arisen in Corinth ('I and not the Lord'). In this application he says that a Christian should not initiate a divorce, but that if the non-Christian partner leaves the marriage, 'let it be so'.

In the circumstances presented, Paul appears to acknowledge that the words of Jesus do not constitute a law or an absolute prohibition of divorce. This saying of Paul, therefore, supports the idea of moral obligations and prescriptive ideals rather than laws, for if Paul saw the words of Jesus as a universal law, it is impossible to understand how he could have claimed the authority to dispense from it. He refrains, however, from spelling out the details of his answer, for in saying, 'let it be so', he does not speak explicitly of remarriage. I suggest that he implies that on that subject his readers should listen to what Jesus had said about powerful prescriptive ideals.

Remarriage

Perhaps recent history shows us why Jesus stopped short of making a law, but did use such forceful and extravagant language in speaking of an ideal. For many centuries in the Christian world all divorce was forbidden, and this caused most serious hardship for large numbers of individuals. Then civil divorce was introduced, at first on very restricted grounds, but eventually, and inevitably, on virtually any ground. The attitudes created by this practice have in their turn affected the manner in which many people approach marriage and the expectations they bring to it, leading to further divorce. Through these attitudes, many people and, of course, many children, are badly hurt. The present situation, in which marriage itself seems to be in danger, can hardly be seen as an ideal by anyone.

I suggest that it is at this point that we can perhaps see why Jesus spoke, not only of the man who divorces his wife and marries another (Mk 10:11; Mt 19:9; Lk 16:18), but also of the woman who is divorced and the man who marries her (Mk 10:12; Mt 5:32; Lk 16:18). We have seen in our own day that, when divorce thoroughly permeates the thinking of a community, and marriage is so little respected that very large numbers of people dispense with it entirely, one of the effects is that married persons are no longer seen as 'off limits'. If one is attracted to a married person, the fact of the marriage often seems to be of little concern in pursuing that attraction. In the thinking of Jesus, such a person has adulterous desires and gives adulterous effect to them, and the married person who responds has equally adulterous desires. Often the other partner is left with little choice other than to agree to the divorce.

At the time of Jesus, women in Israel could not divorce their husbands, but they could put pressure on their husbands to divorce them. If there was an invasion of the marriage by another man, the husband could be left with little choice other than to divorce. In the texts we have been considering, it is obvious that Jesus has gone well beyond the formal act of adultery and has spoken of persons as adulterous when their thinking was adulterous. I have already noted that v 5:32 of Matthew must be interpreted in the light of v 28, where 'looking at a woman with lust' is seen as adultery.

In this sense, the man who has invaded a marriage and the married woman who has responded to him are already adulterous before any act of intercourse has taken place, and certainly before any remarriage occurs. At all times it was not law or external actions that concerned Jesus, but the violation of a solemn commitment of love and the important rights that flowed from this in justice.

I suggest that it was this 'culture' of divorce in his own day that Jesus was seeking to confront. He would not forbid divorce altogether, for this would cause unbearable hardship for some, and in any case he had not come to make a whole series of laws on all subjects. But, with the divorce practice of his own time and place before his eyes, he would have nothing to do with the idea of divorce on any terms and without concern for the harm caused to others or to the institution of marriage itself. The culture of divorce around Jesus was powerful and he had to break through it at all costs and make people think. His response to this dilemma was to call people back to God's original intention in creating male and female and to speak the language of prescriptive ideals, powerful and binding moral obligations that his followers must treat with the utmost seriousness. He would never be content with paying lip service to the idea of permanency while in practice condoning a lax attitude, and so in forceful Semitic language he insisted on total seriousness by presenting the most radical ideal and challenge possible.

When Jesus said, 'If your right eye causes you to sin, tear it out and throw it away', he did not mean this to be taken literally. On the other hand, he certainly did not want anyone to think that it was mere exaggeration and could be ignored. By means of this forceful and concrete language he was saying, 'If something has become an obstacle between you and God, get rid of it. Do whatever you have to do, but get rid of it. Be radical. Treat the matter with the utmost seriousness and accept no compromise.' Instead of using more abstract statements like these, the Semitic Jesus used the more graphic and deliberately shocking pictorial language of tearing out an eye to express the same idea.

I suggest that when he said three verses later, 'Whoever marries a divorced woman commits adultery' he was again using graphic and even shocking pictorial language to express as forcefully as possible the idea that when a marriage is ignored in the pursuit of desire, there is a most serious danger of committing adultery in the heart. He was saying that a man who harboured such thoughts in his heart was in exactly the same position as a man who took a woman from her husband and began living openly with her.

He was insisting that marriage is to be taken with the utmost seriousness, that the words 'for better for worse . . . 'til death do us part' are to be said with all one's heart and soul and being. He was reminding us that we are shaped by the promises we make and the way we stand by them, for they enter into our being and make us the persons we are. He was stressing that, more than almost anything else in human life, the commitment given on a wedding day both expresses and shapes the very persons we are. He was aware of just how much of their happiness and well-being individuals place in the hands of another person on a wedding day, and was insisting that their partners accept this gift as a most sacred trust. He was pointing to the most serious danger of both individuals and whole communities stepping onto the slippery slope that leads to the breakdown of the very institution of marriage.

At the same time, he was acknowledging the seriousness of the difficulties that can arise in marriage. He was acknowledging that situations can occur where separation and divorce are the only intelligent and proper solution. He did his best to combine these two sides to the argument by means of a prescriptive ideal and a commanding, even shocking challenge.

The Ideal

Once we begin to speak the language of prescriptive ideal and commanding challenge rather than law, the vast variety of particular situations that can arise must be taken into account. The words of Jesus, as applied to a man who abandons an older wife and children solely in order to marry a younger one, cannot be applied without further thought to, for example, a woman with young children abandoned by a husband and left destitute.

What was the ideal, then, that Jesus was speaking of in his words about remarriage? Let me start with a case in my pastoral practice. A couple married, but six months later the wife was involved in a car accident that caused serious brain damage and left her unable to communicate or even recognise people. I met the couple some thirty years after this, and found that the man had not remarried but was still devoted to his wife and looking after her every day. He was not a Catholic, so Catholic teachings were not part of his thinking. But he loved his wife and had committed himself to her 'for better for worse, for richer for poorer, in sickness and in health, till death do us part'. I have no desire to make a law for all people out of this free decision of one person, but must we not admit that there was much that is admirable and even heroic in his fidelity? Had not this man in some manner regained the creation?

We may add the not uncommon statement of separated or even divorced persons that 'I couldn't go out with anyone else yet. I still feel married'. When a total commitment was given on a wedding day, many people do not find it easy to leave a marriage behind, no matter what has happened.

When people today talk about divorce, they usually start from the moment when a marriage has completely broken down and ask, 'How should we respond compassionately to this situation?' But Jesus wanted his followers to put this situation into a context. He wanted to ask them, How do you as a young person make sure you yourself are as fully prepared for marriage as your age allows? How should you choose a partner? How seriously do the two of you prepare for your wedding day? How totally do you commit yourselves to each other in that ceremony? How do you live your married life? How do you handle the difficulties that arise? How much are you affected by the culture of divorce around you and how do you respond to it? Do you truly share Christian ideals for marriage and how hard are you willing to work to achieve them? Have you really tried all other alternatives before you even look at separation and divorce? Only in this light can the question of remarriage be seen in context. Only then is the ideal of Jesus still alive. The only people not profoundly hurt by the breakdown of a marriage are those who put little into it in the first place. Jesus was radical and those who genuinely seek to follow him need to be radical, too.

In the light of these considerations, it would seem that for a follower of Jesus, divorce could be accepted in only three cases:

- when a marriage partner has departed and will never return;
- when there is a genuine conflict between the obligations of married life and other more serious obligations, for example, basic obligations towards children or the duty to preserve one's own life and sanity;
- when, despite all efforts, including the seeking of assistance from others through counselling, the living of anything that could be called 'married life' has become an impossibility.

It is in interpreting these three criteria and applying them to a particular situation that the strength of the challenge of Jesus would have to be kept firmly in mind.

Is this combination of prescriptive ideal and radical and shocking challenge more in conformity with everything we know about the *person* of Jesus Christ than the idea of his using divine authority to decree a law? Is it in conformity with the story of his own life and death on a cross? On this basis can we reconcile the words of the gospels with all we know about the *person* who spoke them?

Three Further Considerations

1. We know that Jesus repeatedly insisted on a proper handling of authority within the community, and yet the Church seems to have brushed aside his advice to call no one father or teacher with little difficulty. He spoke against taking oaths, yet they are routine in the Church. He said very little about sex, and yet the Church has insisted on sexual morality more than on the love and social justice

in human affairs that was a constant and powerful theme of the teaching of Jesus. All that I said about sex in the previous chapter is also relevant here. In looking at the whole question of marriage and divorce, we must surely go back to the priorities of Jesus.

2. The early Church, and even Jesus himself, believed that the world and all its institutions would end in the very near future. There is even a tension between earlier and later parts of the Second Testament on this point. It follows that the entire social situation in which marriage must be lived is not without relevance when considering matters of marriage and divorce.

3. The Catholic Church is not as 'imprisoned' in Scripture as the Churches of the Reformation. A *living* tradition, inspired by the Spirit, has always been recognised as an interpretative principle.

Conclusion

It is obvious that, even for those Christians who most earnestly seek the will of Jesus in this matter of divorce and remarriage, there are many problems in the evidence of the Second Testament, for uncertainties abound in every single one of the texts. Is this an indication that, while we must have the greatest respect for the Scriptures, God will not solve all our problems for us, and we cannot put all the responsibility onto God? Must we not rather take a large measure of both personal and collective responsibility in this delicate and difficult field?

I fear that some Protestant Churches have in practice been caught into ways of acting on this subject that do not do justice to the powerful call of Jesus. At the same time there must be queries as to whether the teaching of the Catholic Church, as set out in canons 5 and 7 of the Canons on the Sacrament of Matrimony of the Council of Trent,[30] truly respects the teaching and the *person* of Jesus as revealed to us in the Second Testament. I hope that I have shown that these canons of Trent are selective in the parts of the Second Testament they quote and fall well short of reflecting the entirety of the evidence. Surely there are matters here that are in urgent need of serious discussion.

---

30. '5. *If anyone says that the marriage bond can be dissolved because of heresy, or irksome cohabitation, or because of the wilful desertion of one of the spouses, anathema sit . . . 7. If anyone says that the Church is in error for having taught and for still teaching that in accordance with the evangelical and apostolic doctrine (cf Mk10:1; 1Cor 7), the marriage bond cannot be dissolved because of adultery on the part of one of the spouses, and that neither of the two, not even the innocent one who has given no cause for infidelity, can contract another marriage during the lifetime of the other; and that the husband who dismisses an adulterous wife and marries again and the wife who dismisses an adulterous husband and marries again are both guilty of adultery, anathema sit.'* Quoted from *The Christian Faith in the Doctrinal Documents of the Catholic Church*, Edited by J Neuner and J Dupuis (London: Collins Liturgical Publications, 1983), 529.

3

The Development of Doctrine

A number of people will accuse me of violating solemn and, indeed, infallible teachings in what I have written in the last two chapters, so that is the question I must now address.

At the end of the last chapter I quoted in a footnote the canons of the Council of Trent on the subject of divorce, and this would certainly be held to be infallible teaching. The status of the general teaching on sexual morality is not as clear, and yet in chapter One I quoted in a footnote two popes who said that anyone who denied that teaching should be referred to the Inquisition. At the very least it would be considered definitive teaching many times repeated and would be insisted upon as though it were infallible. So how can there be a contrary opinion on either subject? By what right can I claim that the matters may even be discussed?

The problem is perhaps clearer in relation to divorce. I invite the reader to put aside for a moment the teaching of Trent and look at what I have written simply in terms of scripture. If, after studying it carefully according to all the rules of scriptural interpretation, you reject what I have written, then you have no problem and Trent reigns supreme for you. But if you find that the arguments given there have a serious foundation, then you have a true dilemma, for then scripture would seem to be saying one thing and the Council of Trent another. Both scripture and a solemn ecumenical council are massive authorities, so how does one resolve this dilemma?

Some would reply that this is precisely why the teaching authority of the Church exists, for it authoritatively interprets scripture for us. They hold that what we must believe is scripture interpreted for us by the Church. But others would not be happy with this view, not wishing to put scripture aside so easily, for surely Church teaching must be based on scripture and may not contradict it. Is there a solution to this dilemma?

The Second Vatican Council

The Second Vatican Council (1962–65) faced a tension between the need to be faithful to its origins and the need to confront the pastoral problems posed by the modern world. The solution the Vatican Council found was in the combination of two words, one Italian and one French. The Italian word was *aggiornamento*, meaning 'bringing up to date'; the French word was *ressourcement*, meaning 'going back to the sources'. The council sought to bring the Church up to date, not by confronting the immediate past head on, but by going back to a far older tradition based on scripture and the teachings of the ancient Fathers.

It followed a principle that one writer has called 'discontinuity for the sake of a greater continuity',[1] that is, in attempting to reconcile opposing views the council often reached back behind a particular formulation of truth to an earlier and greater truth. For example, the council:

-      went behind the Scholastic categories that had dominated for a thousand years to the riches of the early Fathers of the Church;
-      went behind the static neo-Scholastic categories of the Church as a 'perfect society' to a more dynamic concept of a pilgrim Church on a journey and involved in history;
-      went behind the second millennium's emphasis on hierarchy to the first millennium's greater balance between hierarchy and communion;

---

1.   Ormond Rush, *Still Interpreting Vatican II, Some Hermeneutical Principles* (New York: Paulist Press, 2004).

- went behind a thousand years of exclusively clerical decision-making on all matters of faith to revive the ancient idea of the *sensus fidei*, the 'sense of faith' of the whole people of God;

- went behind a thousand years of teaching that a bishop's power of governance came from the pope to the idea that all of a bishop's power comes from ordination;

- went behind many centuries of teaching that only truth has rights to the idea that it is people who have rights, even when they are in error;

- went behind much of both the first and second millennium to a rejection of the idea of 'Christendom';

- went behind Gregory VII's virtual rejection of the bishops in his confrontation with the emperor in the eleventh century to a teaching concerning the college of bishops as an equal holder of supreme power within the Church;

- went behind the Council of Trent and the whole Counter-Reformation to an appreciation of the independent reception of the Great Tradition by the separated churches and to open dialogue with them;

- went behind the same Council of Trent and Counter-Reformation to a better balance between Scripture and Tradition in the life of the Church;

- went behind the negative attitudes and style of Gregory XVI, Pius IX and Pius X in their condemnations of 'modernity' in the nineteenth and early twentieth centuries to the sentiments expressed in the first sentence of *Gaudium et Spes*: '*The joy and hope, the grief and anguish of the people of our time, especially of those who are poor or afflicted in any way, are the joy and hope, the grief and anguish of the followers of Christ as well. Nothing that is genuinely human fails to find an echo in their hearts.*'[2]

---

2.   Second Vatican Council, *Pastoral Constitution on the Church in the Modern World*, no 1.

In following this method, the Second Vatican Council achieved remarkable results. Among the irreversible fruits of the Council are that:

- it saw the Church as a divine mystery and a pilgrim people rather than simply as a hierarchical institution or 'perfect society',
- it placed the bible back beside the sacraments at the centre of Church life, and opened up the bible to a deeper understanding,
- it put the pope into the context of the college of bishops,
- it greatly promoted the active role of the laity,
- it renewed enthusiasm for Christian unity,
- it brought some settlement to ancient tensions between Christians and Jews,
- it made landmark and, for some, radical, statements on religious liberty and conscience,
- it brought the liturgy to the people.

In doing all of this, it modified statements and traditions that had been in place for centuries. It did this despite the fact that, with considerable heat and fury, this trend was constantly and adamantly condemned by a number of members of the Council.

Ressourcement

If we follow the Second Vatican Council's principle of *ressourcememt*, we may quote some very influential sources. St Augustine wrote:

> *The writings of bishops may be refuted both by the perhaps wiser words of anyone more experienced in the matter and by the weightier authority and more scholarly prudence of other bishops, and also by councils, if something in them perhaps has deviated from the truth; even councils held in particular regions or provinces must without quibbling give way to the authority of plenary councils of*

the whole Christian world; and even the earlier plenary councils are often corrected by later ones, if as a result of practical experience something that was closed is opened, something that was hidden becomes known.[3]

One hundred and fifty years later Pope Pelagius II made a statement that had been drafted by a deacon of his household who, on his death, became Pope Gregory the Great. The document said:

Dear brethren, do you think that when Peter was reversing his position, one should have replied: We refuse to hear what you are saying since you previously taught the opposite? In the matter [now under discussion] one position was held while truth was being sought, and a different position was adopted after truth had been found. Why should a change of position be thought a crime . . .? For what is reprehensible is not changing one's mind, but being fickle in one's views. If the mind remains unwavering in seeking to know what is right, why should you object when it abandons its ignorance and reformulates its views?[4]

Do not both of these statements seem extremely reasonable? On other subjects both St Augustine and St Gregory the Great have massive influence when arguing for a particular teaching, so why not here?

Contradicting Versus Modifying

In the last two chapters I have not argued for the exact opposite of earlier teaching. On sexual morality I am far from arguing for 'anything goes' or 'do as you like' or even the idea of 'do no harm'. I

---

3. St Augustine, *De baptismo contra Donatistas,* Book III, chapter 2. The words I have quoted have been omitted from some editions, but I am assured that they belong there.
4. Quoted by Robert Markus, emeritus professor of history at Nottingham University, in a review of the book *Papal Sin, Structures of Deceit* by Gary Wills, in *The Tablet,* 2nd September 2000.

strongly insist that all sexual acts must be based on the fundamental principle of Jesus that we should always and in all circumstances 'love our neighbour'.

On the subject of divorce, I am certainly not advocating casual divorce. I strongly emphasise the powerful words of Jesus concerning the commitment to permanence and the serious work demanded to ensure that a marriage does in fact flourish and last. If I have difficulties with the idea of indissolubility on the lips of Jesus, I do find permanence to be something that he stressed in the most powerful language at his command.

I note also that the argument of Jesus in Mark and Matthew is itself a classic example of *ressourcement*, for he based his entire argument on the call to 'regain the creation', that is, 'to return to the sources', to sweep aside all human additions and live marriage as God in creation intended it to be for the good of individuals and the whole human race.

On the subject of infallibility, I am certainly not suggesting that we deny altogether the idea of authoritative teaching in the Church. All I suggest is that we accept the surely reasonable principle that a later general council of the Church should have the authority to modify or clarify or adapt the teaching of an earlier general council in the light of developing knowledge and understanding. This is far from being something new, for it is exactly what happened in the field of Christology over a series of seven Councils from Nicaea (325) to Nicaea II (787), as understanding was purified and improved.

In relation to sexual morality, the modifications are that we should move from the idea of sexual offences being offences directly against God to Jesus' own idea of offences against others, especially 'little ones', moving God profoundly; from a morality of physical acts to a morality of acts of persons; from a more abstract concept of 'natural acts' to a morality based on what is in fact natural to different people; and from philosophical argument to a greater combination of reason and Scripture.

In relation to divorce, the modification is that we should move from the idea of a legal bond created by God to a powerful moral bond created by the couple themselves and strongly approved and endorsed by Jesus.

In relation to infallibility itself, the modification is that we should allow for legitimate, necessary and inevitable development by permitting that an authority equal to the earlier authority should have the power to make modifications to earlier teaching.

In the terms used by the Second Vatican Council, I am arguing for *ressourcememt*, a going back to earlier sources. I am arguing for *aggiornamento*, a bringing up to date in the light of further study of the scriptures. And I am arguing for 'discontinuity for the sake of a greater continuity'. Without this the concept of 'development of doctrine' becomes nearly impossible.

In this I am not arguing for anything more than the Second Vatican Council itself has already done in a number of different fields.

If we deny this, the Church will be unable to move forwards, even when it becomes clear that it should do so, for it will not even be able to make modifications to earlier teaching.

If we deny it for the two issues raised—divorced persons and homosexuals—we will never find an adequate solution to their pastoral needs. We will have two large groups of people within the Church whose pastoral needs we admit we cannot meet. Can a Christian church accept this?

We have a vast distance to travel before we can return the world to the love from which it came. This early in that journey, it would be most unwise to allow the past to bind the future in bonds so tight that they not merely cannot ever be taken away, but cannot even be modified or adapted to new circumstances.

Of course Church Councils produce truth, but is it eternal and unchangeable truth, or is it, even with divine assistance, the best possible truth a particular Church Council is capable of within the limits that surround any human endeavour? Should we now do our best to produce the best possible truth we are capable of at this time in our history concerning the divorced and homosexuals?

Every bishop has at some stage tried to have a conversation with one or more young people on the subject of sexual morality and found that, even when real good will is present, they cannot accept ideas of 'natural purposes of natural acts' as a serious basis for a whole sexual morality. The same is true of teaching on divorce, particularly since most Catholic people today have a relative or friend whose marriage has failed. They are convinced that the teaching of Trent on divorce could not have come from the Jesus they have come to know. We have reached a point where conversation has dried up, and all that is left is for the bishop to insist on infallible teaching to an audience that is no longer listening.

May I suggest that the great advantage of what I have proposed in the last two chapters is that on this basis the entire conversation could be renewed. At last we could actually have a conversation with young people in which we both listened and spoke. I suggest that Catholic people would be very accepting of the proposal that ideas such as 'anything goes' or 'do what you like' are a poor basis for living, and that they would see the dangers of adopting only the idea of 'do no harm'. Would it not be wonderful to be able finally to have this real conversation! At last Jesus, Church authority and Catholic people would be in the same room and talking the same language!

The same would be true of divorce. People would be willing to accept that Jesus had made powerful statements about commitment and permanence. They are also aware that casual divorce puts marriage itself at risk and is no way into the future.

I note that a Church Synod could not make these decisions, for only a council of equal stature could modify the views of an earlier council, so the new Church Council would have to be equal to that of Trent in every way. The question before the Synod, I suggest, is whether to advise Pope Francis to call such a Church Council or not.

It is possible to have a shorter council that discusses only two or three topics. There is no necessity that it be as grand as Vatican II or Trent.

The emperor and the kings of France and Spain, all lay persons, were most powerful and influential forces at Trent, and I make a plea that the laity be fully part of and directly represented at this council, for example, for every bishop there be also a lay representative with full voting rights.

This would be possible, for much of the Council could be conducted on the internet.

One effect of the abuse crisis is that the bishops have lost a vast amount of authority and credibility before the whole world and in the eyes of the Catholic people themselves. On the subjects of sex, gender and marriage they desperately need the laity. The bishops in Council may believe that they speak with authority, but it is only together with the laity that they can speak with credibility, and, therefore, with true authority.

Epilogue

The promise of Jesus Christ was not that the Church will never
make mistakes,
but that it will overcome its mistakes,
for the truth of Jesus Christ will always be present in the Church
—tarnished and even obscured—
but always there to be rediscovered.

The promise is that, in spite of many errors in detail,
the Church will be maintained in the basic truth of the Song of
Jesus,
and that the ugliness in the Church
will never completely destroy its underlying beauty.

'The Church's faith will often be weak, its love lukewarm, its hope
wavering,
but that on which its faith is based, its love is rooted and its hope
is built
will always endure.'[1]

There is a certainty of faith,
though it is certainty in something that comes before words.
It is the certainty of faith in the teacher and his song!

There was a teacher and he sang a song.
The teacher was inspiring,
and his song of love makes my heart sing—
this I believe with certainty.

No other certainty can be equal to this certainty,
and it is by tortuous paths,
and through many uncertainties,
that we must humbly and hesitantly
seek to return the world to the love from which it came.

---

1.   Hans Kung, *Infallible?* (Collins Fontana Library, 1970), 153.

Biblical Index

CPSIA information can be obtained at www.ICGtesting.com
Printed in the USA
BVOW05s1620160415

396493BV00002B/118/P